Running Country

NEHEMY N. KIHARA

ISBN: 1540346617
ISBN-13:9781540346612

DEDICATION

Above all the book is dedicated to
Janduong (Elder),the late
H.E. Jaramogi Oginga Odinga, a Nation Founding Father
and the First Vice President of Kenya,
who persistently fought for Liberty and Justice.

Dedicated to my former teaching colleague at Kenyatta University,
the late Prof Wamere—Mwangi-Dadet,
longtime Head of the French and Foreign Languages Department.
An Activist /Educator with whom we faced the KANU
Parliamentary Commission -Central Province Hearings at Nyeri, with
Critical Educational Reforms Proposals ; and with a few others) we
were able to maintain through a long lasting 'strike' the flames of
banned University Academic and Staff Unin ,

Dedicated also to my fellow Clergy-
the Rev.Dr.Timothy Njoya Murere, Ph.D.
a Cutting Edge Theologian/Political Activist and Reformer; with
whom we were able to present "Proposals for Reforms" to the
KANU Review Committee sitting at Nyeri
-Central Provincial Headquarters.

CONTENTS

ACKNOWLEDGMENTS

I am grateful to all freedom fighters who inspired me to always struggle for the uplifting the lives of the least in our communities..

1 INTRODUCTION

Generally, at the beginning of the modern era, there were People in east Africa, with elaborate social institutions and civilization of a non-western type. While little is known of the interior parts of east Africa, there has been considerable evidence of the coast people and their long contacts and relationships with the rest of the world.

Early traders from Arabia, Assyria, Egypt, Greece, India, Persia, and Phoenicia are known to have visited the coast during the Pre-Christian period, and some of these settled there.

Therefore, Kenya was somehow connected with the rest of the world even before the colonial period.

Another thing that one needs to understand is that geographical names have changed. Many of the names one finds in an Atlas reminiscent of colonial times have changed to a great extent.

Aberdares now is called Nyandarua Mountain.

Lake Bogoria replaced Hannington,

Hoy's Bridge became Moi's Bridge,

Lake Rudolf is now Lake Turkana.

Towns like Fort Hall, now Muranga

Thomson's Falls became Nyahururu

It seems proper for one to make sure they have a map that represents some of these post-independence period.

The African continent in general and Kenya in particular is always changing and this process is noted not only by historical, ideological and ecological but also in geo-political conditions.

THE COUNTRY

The Republic of Kenya, with Nairobi as its capital, consists of an area of about 224,960 square miles, with a population estimated (1986) to be about 20 millions. This will double to 40 million by 2010. It is bordered on the north by Sudan, Ethiopia and Somalia, the Indian Ocean on the east coast, Tanzania on the south and Uganda on the west.

Language/Ethnicity:

The country uses Swahili as its national language but English is widely spoken. Other ethnic languages are used in different areas of the country. Amongst the majority of Kenya's 70 ethnolinguistic groups are the Agem - Agikuyu, Embu and Meru (over quarter of the population; and Abaluhya, Luo, A-Kamba, Kalenjin, over one million each. The minority groups include Arabs, Asians, and Euros.

Agriculture serves as the backbone of the economy but there is a growing industrial sector (mostly manufacturing).

Devolved Counties: Kenya administered through 47 counties(formerly districts) It was formerly divided into eight provinces which include Nairobi, Central, Coastal, Eastern, Northern Eastern, Nyanza, Rift Valley and Western.

Politics: The government is headed by the [Rais] President assisted by a [Makamu] Vice-President, on the Executive branch[Serikali].

The Legislative branch[Bunge] consists of a unicameral national Assembly of 188 members and the

Attorney General[Mkuu-wa-Sheria]. The Judicial branch[Sheria] includes the highest Court of Appeals[Kodhi-Kuu] headed by the Chief Justice, the High Court and two subordinate courts the resident and district magistrate courts.

The Islamic Kadis-courts hear cases concerning Moslem laws. Kenya was a one party state with the ruling Kenya African National Union (KANU) headed by the President until late 1990s.

Migration: There has been frequent migration of pastoralists from the north and northwest seeking water and grass and of agriculturalists from the east and southeast who occupied the fertile and highland areas.

According to "genesis stories" or oral traditions of those who lived in the central part of the country, their original place was either where they presently live, the north or from further south in the direction of Tanzania or from the coast, especially near present day Lamu, in a place called Sinyanga.

Origin: The country got its present name from Mount Kirinyaga or the Mountain of Brightness, which is surrounded by the Bantu speaking people of Gikuyu-Chuka, Embu, Mbeere, Ndia and Meru-Igembe, Igonji, Imenti, Muimbi, Muthambe, Tharaka, Tigania, and A-Kamba.

An European traveler exploring the interior sighted the mountain in 1849. Upon inquiry of its local name, the Kamba companions informed him that it is KIINYAA and out of that Kenya was derived.

World Contact: It was from the coast that Europeans penetrated the interior of the country, in which Mombasa and Malindi were main city-states. Vasco da Gama in 1498 on his way to India, not only was a famous Portuguese visitor but a key factor in capturing the town of Mombasa by the Portuguese and building their defensive stronghold.

The Arabs ruled it through Mazrui whose rule was ended by the Omani Sultan Sayyid Said of the Busaidi dynasty in 1937. The Sultan moved his Muscat headquarters to Zanzibar. Mombasa by 1824 to 1826 had been set up as a protectorate by a British Captain Owen.

The missionary adventures, were marked by the establishment of Rabai Station in 1844 at Malindi by Dr. John Kraft, of the Church Missionary Society. Kraft and Rebman were credited with being the first white men to see Mount Kenya (Kirinyaga)

These missionaries and other European explorers who began to penetrate the interior in the middle of 19th century set the stage for colonization. By 1884-5 at a Berlin Conference the partitioning of Africa had been already laid down. By 1886 Kenya, which had been given to British East African Imperial company, had entered the colonial era,

Kenya is known in the whole world as the "Country of Runners" due to the fact that it has dominated the world in middle distance and marathon races, both for men and women.

Predominantly, the Kalenjin community from the highlands of Rift Valley, made the core of its champions. From such great Olympians as Kipchoge Keino to the current world record holders.

However, recently we've had champions from the Agikuyu community, such Gold Medalists as Wanjiru and Ndereba ;as well as Waruingi known for Boxing, from the Mount Kenya highlands; as well as the Akamba, well known for Archery and Sharp Shooting, from the Eastern Plains and Abagusii of Western highlands; making their mark in Field and Track Sports.

In other sports are the Joluo and Abaluhya communities of the West-Counties dominating Soccer, Rugby and Boxing, such as Gold Medalist Wangila).

Many other communities like the Maasai and Turkana have been known for their sports skills and have done well in Olympics like Gold Medalist Rudisha.

In this book, however, we examine the Nation on the basis of another race, the drive to develop a country .Kenya has always been on the run ,since independence as a multiparty state, one party dictatorship stained by nepotism and corruption ,then a democratizing multi-party state.

Kenya has been a Republic since 1964 and to ask such a question may seem odd to some but the contemporary political and socio-economic structures in which the development (or Maendeleo) process takes place renders such a question to be relevant. Any national planning should be asking this question in order to be involved in a dynamic process of development.

In order to respond to the question, I will attempt to discuss three points: First, what sort of society we have built thus far: (Historical Reflection: Colonialism to Independent Struggle;] secondly, what kind of society we are today: (An Ethical Critique of Capitalist (Maendeleo) Development;] Thirdly, what society we should be building towards year 2050 and beyond.: [Socialist Alternatives].

Although by the virtue of my areas of scholarly training and academic interests, I am a social scientist; I am also by all means and in practice an African theologian.

Therefore, as a social scientist I will strive to be as much objective as possible in my analysis, but as an African theologian, be true to my commitment to "traditional socio-cultural values", which obviously will force me to a certain amount of subjectivity.

It is from this more or less marginal and interdisciplinary perspective that I will attempt my critical analysis and ideological reflection on "Kenya Towards Year 2050 A.D. and Beyond."

2 COLONIAL CAPITALIST DEVELOPMENT

Colonialism: The process of colonization started with a few European explorers, accompanied by African from the interior, in trade contact with the coast. This involved a larger number of coastal people, including Arabs.

Previously, trade involved these groups with cargo to European markets of ivory and slaves. Such trade involved certain chieftains and Arabs collaborating in an exchange system.

The imperial domination of Europeans not only involved these politico-economic factors but also religious ones, in which the Christian missionaries were central actors.

The establishment of European rule, coincided with rise of Christian missions, presumably committed to conversion and relief measures to eradicate slavery, sickness, and ignorance.

The British government took over the British East African Company. In 1902, this protectorate was enlarged, and a railway linkage with Uganda established. In 1920 the country became a crown colony known as the Kenya colony.

The railway building which linked Mombasa to the interior had brought a migration of Indians who stayed to become traders and dominated the commercial interests of Kenya.

The colonial government also encouraged the settlement of Europeans and some south African Boers - (veterans of World War I) ont he best land in the highlands which displaced the Gikuyu people and restricted the activities of their traditional neighbors, the Maasai.

These European settlers were the dominant voice in the colonial government. The missionaries and administrators gained more influence as the system extended into public affairs and social services.

Since 1920 when Kenya became a colony of the British Empire, the European colonialists in the form of "white settlers" had established themselves as a powerful economic and political minority.

Not only had they benefitted from the treacherous theft of our best and productive land, but they had turned us into laborers in their thousands and thousands acres of farm land.

Consolidation of Neo-Colonialism

1980 comes to an end, and year 1981 comes to the scene, Kenya becomes a concern for the international community in general, and the whole continent of Africa in particular.

First of all, 1981 brings the chairmanship of O.A.U. to our Head of State "Raisi" making the Republic in one way or the other the focal point of Continental conflicts (where nations in conflict will rally for "peaceful resolutions").

Secondly, the responsibilities of the "international community" of which Kenya carries a bigger portion, with a number of U.N. programs in one country will bring us closer to global scrutiny of our land, people and policy.

The two developments, although external, may bring our internal problems more and more to the open, despite "Serikali (government) measures" to present to the world a more brighter picture of our national stability.

Furthermore, our socio-political and economic situation according to recent reports, does reveal that despite various explanations by our leaders about the so-called "mixed economy" our development policy has drifted more and more towards corporate and transnational capitalism.

What we've been calling development is in disguise a "Capitalist Maendeleo" or progress towards capitalism. At this juncture I would like us to reflect a bit on our historical situation.

3 AFRICAN CAPITALIST DEVELOPMENT

Africans or Kenyans had become mere means of labor-producing capital, not only for the appetites of these "Bwana Mkubwas" (big lords), but also for their sponsors and kinships, the royal British Crown and its subjects.

Any reasonable and logical attempt to make these come to their senses was useless. They had the land-economic power and its political apparatus was at their disposal and could be used at any time.

However, our people, thanks to God ,opted of a revolutionary action. They rose up and took up their arms immediately after World War II and decided to set into motion a painful liberation struggle which for a decade made the colonialists and white settlers dream (to turn Kenya into a "white haven") unrealistic if not completely impossible.

For those whom the struggle for independence seems just like a mere incidence better characterized by terrorist activities and tribal warfare (amongst the Gikuyu's), it is easier to forget and also urge the rest of us in distinguish of national unity and peace to bury these 15 years of liberation struggle, into the past, so as to concentrate on the future.

To me to forget such an important period in our history is paramount to forgetting all these years we've been an independent nation.

The realities of the 1950's were very harsh to the population concerned.
Some of us were affected more than others; others worked in collaboration with the enemy , the Britons , yet we were all yearning for freedom and survival.

We know the realities of that period, some were not yet born, yet these realities are hard to bury. Without "telling the truth" there can be no forgiveness or national reconciliation. Mzee Jomo Kenyatta hit a good balance of this situation when he declared "Kusameheana twawesa kuwasemehea, lakini hatuwesi kusahau."

Of course, we understand that within the contradictions to be found in a struggle like the one our nation underwent, were those who collaborated with the colonizers, the homeguard types and the rest.

But to save the shame of a few of our kin, a whole nation's pride in its revolution towards freedom and ever-present will to change oppressive structures (socio-economic

4 AFRICAN UNDERMINED FREEDOM

It is my feeling that by deemphasizing the fact that someone laid their lives for our freedom undermines our very pride as a revolutionary African nation, like Algeria, Mozambique, Angola and the rest that smashed the dreams of the colonizers and doomed their empire extension in the African continent forever.

Revolutionary action, therefore, can be considered a Kenyan historical characteristic in which our people can always resort to when mere reforms can no longer help meet their basic needs or bring structural changes into the production and just distribution of goods and services.

Any public and socio-economic policy that deviates from this historical character or makes us think that we are nothing less than products of British structures, children of the commonwealth and by-products of missionary piety.

Such assumptions merely insults the intellect and the will of our people to be totally liberated and free to enjoy the land that is by all human rights "our own".

A truly Kenyan development would be based on this historical reality that our independence was not handed to us after a merry dancing match or beer party in a western Europe capital city.

Kenyan liberty, "Uhuru" (freedom) was won out of a bitter liberation struggle in which masses of people lost their lives in the villages and the lonely and scaring forests surrounding Mount Kenya where the Land Freedom Army waged a guerilla warfare until victory was certain.

How can we as a people forget these harsh realities that characterized the birth or our nation "Hatuwesi Kusahau". As long as ours remains an independent nation, no one ought to forget how that precious freedom was won.

Today we find most of us laughing, dancing and even marrying our former (Britons) colonial masters. Even you will find us electing them to represent us in the Parliament and Senate and County Governments.

What matters most to many of us, is ("ni yule ana pesa") the one with money, or even have them as the highest advisors and policy planners in our government ministries.

However, let us not forget that theirs was not a dream of just becoming one of us "wananchi", but it was a master plan to make us inferior colonial subjects forever.

The separate development "multiracial" claim of South Africa, where most of Kenyan settlers population went, after Kenyan independence..

This was a reminder of what our society could have been if our oppressed people did not radically oppose the colonial policy.

Freedom fighters opted to sacrifice their lives and that of their relatives for an independence, freedom and land some of them never enjoyed.

Most of these had to bite the dust before victory was won.

Nation-Building: In 1965 a freedom fighter, trade unionist and member of Parliament, Pinto (Goan Indian) was assassinated, the following year the Vice-President, Oginga Odinga, a leading JALUO nationalist and veteran freedom fighter, resigned to form an opposition Kenya Peoples Union. This was later banned and Oginga detained from 1969 to 1971. Another JALUO and Minister of Economist Planning Tom Mboya was assassinated in 1969 (as the second member of Parliament).

The 1970's saw the inauguration of the University of Nairobi, and he second National Elections in 1974. The third member of Parliament (a Gikuyu), J.M. Kariuku, popular government critic and former MAU MAU detainee, was assassinated in 1975. In 1978, the founding father of the nation Jomo Kenyatta died and was succeeded by Vice-President Arap Moi, who was confirmed in 1979, as the President. Kenya experienced an attempted but unsuccessful coup by the Air Force in 1982. A general election was held in 1983 with some changes in policy or direction.

Within the next few years the supremacy of KANU the ruling party

and mass participation began to be felt. As the country started a race

of   development   "Kenya   is   still   on   the   run".

5 STRUGGLE TOWARDS INDEPENDENCE

Nationalism: African nationalism challenged the colonial policy of racial segregation, demanded the return of stolen lands and proper and effective representation.

The legitimacy of the European settlers to dominate the Africans was also challenged. By the 1940's, all African Associations had been proscribed.

The Gikuyu had begun nationalist movements as early as 1919. This resulted in the deportation of its leader, Harry Thuku, for nine years in Kisimayu (Somalia). The Luos and Kambas had also begun some movements.

For the first time an African was nominated to the Legislative Council in 1944. Previously their interests were represented without their mandate by missionaries: in 1924 J.W. Arthur (Church of Scotland) and in 1943 by Rev. L.J. Beecher) (Church of England).

Meanwhile, Kenyatta, who was associated with anti-missionary Kenya African Teachers Training College and Kikuyu Karinga (Orthodox) Church, was main the demands of Africans heard in the fifth Pan African Congress in Manchester in 1945. Two years later he become the President of Kenya African Union, which had grown out of a study group.

Protest and Resistance: Trade unionism became another vocal rallying pint for African interests with Fred Kubai and Makham Singh at the forefront.

By the late 1940's the growing African opposition amongst the Gikuyu developed the Party which through an "oath of unity" became the Military Action Unit of the Movement for African Unity (alias MAU MAU).

The Land Freedom Army was predominantly Gikuyu in composition, partly because the location of its struggle was in the "white highlands" which were considered "stolen Gikuyu lands" from which they were displaced.

In this case Gikuyu, the most numerous of Kenya people, were more directly affected by colonial and settler's policy than others. Moreover, other ethnic groups were involved in the guerrilla struggle, the immediate relatives, the Meru, and Kamba; and Maasai and their distant allies, others because of their extreme borders and locations could not do more than political and moral support.

The armed struggle was marked by the beginning of an emergency in October, 1952, and ended, according to British records, in 1956 with the capture and execution of Dedan Kimathi, one of the Field Marshals of the Land Freedom Army (and its central commander).

However, contrary to those colonial records the Movement never ceased to exist, it was just weakened by internal political developments and colonial government repressions and restrictive measures. The majority of African agitators for freedom were in detention, including Kenyatta, the most visible nationalist.

The labor movement and civil, urban agitation dominated by the Luo and the Gikuyu continued the struggle which resulted in the foundation of Kenya African National Union (formerly KAU) and its opposing Kenya African Democratic Union, which demanded a regional independence, and the Kenya Freedom Party by Asians.

During our "struggle for independence" we were clear about the true nature of European rule "Utawala wa Wangeleza" which was based on a pure profit making and selfish capitalist motive.

This in practice justified the oppression of thousands of labourers by one white settler, whose main job was only to "kufungua mudomo" command and unveil the colonial development plans, then the production machine (African Kenya labor) was put into motion.

These British administrators and settlers with the benefits of modern technology made us think they were genius and we were nothing less than dummies.

To them the average Africans were better colonized, if the British did not do it the Arabs and Asians could as well have done it.

In fact the average "white settler" thought in a very limited sense,

he could not have an African (Kenyan dark skinned person) to have acted contrary to the colonizers handbook "stereotyped"; when independence finally came some of them were unprepared to face "Black rule".

Even Prince Charles, I understand, was urging, then to be, Prime Minister -Kenyatta, to change his mind while there was time , before the Union Jack went down to let the Kenyan Black, Red and Green and white flag to rise to the sky.

Kenyatta said "No" and the pink man image of the African seemed to have begun a radical transformation.

Unfortunately, when we gained our independence, not only did we inherit the British system of socio-economic development, but it seems, after 17 years of independence as if we deliberately opted to retain it in the pretext of "mixed economy".

To our comfort we might as well admit that we were unable to break away from it, due to our lack of an ideological base or foundation for an integral human development.

6 ETHICAL CRITIQUE

Ideology: The nation's ideological stance is capitalist with a philosophy called Nyayo (footsteps Following) which is based on love, peace and unity. Nyayoism stresses continuity of the idea of Harambee (pulling Together) which the late President Kenyatta emphasized and H.E. arap Moi, the new President, has pledged to follow.

As far as the politico-economic stability of the nation is concerned, recent events show signs of recovery on the surface yet deep problems could be ignited by the continuation of economic inequality, corruption in high places and external dependency.

During our struggle for independence our ideology was based on "Land and Freedom" the goal was as clear as the path to attain it. After independence freedom was at our disposal, so was the land. Harambee became the action orienting ideology.

We had to "pull together" but how far remained a constant question after Mzee was gone. Now "Nyayo" following the footsteps has become yet another philosophical rhetoric.

But one question still haunts us ; Whose footsteps should be followed? 'Rais Aliyopo', the present President or ' au'the "Late Mzee".

"Kusifuata Nyayo" or in order to follow the footsteps do we need to go into the past for the sake of continuity, which might result into regression or do we follow someone forward, guiding us into the future which means progress.

May be the "Nyayo" philosophy of Love, Peace and Unity will become clear as time constantly tests its premises.

But if Nyayo means following Raisi Aliyopo.Hon. Arap Moi", his first year in office seems to point towards progress he has visited almost all of the 8 Provinces in the Republic, free primary education and the setting free of political detainees and prisoners have been witnessed.

It seems that under Moi the repressive measures that had characterized our nation as someone took the reigns of the government behind the "Aging Mzee", where some critics of the policy had been imprisoned without trial had for a while diminished.

However, despite the credit that all of us can give the Kenyan Republic, since independence, it seems fair that we should equally give it a constructive critique.

It seems clear to most of us after the past seventeen years, that the very system that we fought to break from has eventually become our development model.

Moreover, before our independence to have opted to a capitalist post-independent, development would have been to blindly opt to be permanently glued to the colonial structures, that have for so long oppressed us and doomed our destiny.

Yet an evaluation of our contemporary socio-economic development since independence tends to strongly suggest that our planning and policies are still based very much on a neo-colonial structure, that in essence works to preserve the interests of the imperialists and capitalists of the Western Europe

7 DEVELOPMENT: CAPITALIST OR SOCIALIST

As an economic developmental model, capitalism may work better for those Western European countries with enough capital (e.g. U.S.A., British and their NATO allies).

Moreover, as a third world African nation with over 88% of the population living under subsistence economy in the rural areas, the system does not fit our conditions.

Maendeleo or Progression "Development" in Kenya has been following a capitalist path that continuity generates more wealth for the few "Matajiri" rich, while it continues to create mass misery and inequality.

This sort of unequal concentration of capital and technology in the hands of few has resulted into a crisis in our economy.

A lot of talk about law and order and anticommunist rhetoric can now be heard in the 1970s and 80s which call for tough measures to curb foreign ideologies.

As far as I am concerned, the most undesirable foreign ideology is not Chinese Development, otherwise if it is not good for us, the recent presidential visit to that country was not be necessary; nor a Soviet Development, otherwise the planned Presidential visit Russia should be cancelled.

The author never advocated for Chinese or Soviet Development for our country, but to put his observation in perspective, what he is merely saying is that any condemnation of foreign ideologies should have started with where Kenyan economy has reached.

Western Corporate Capitalism ,that seems to be 'foreign of all ideologies' which are supposed to be our enemy, at this stage of development.

Imagine a developing country with 48 million people in 2016 already with hundreds of transnational corporations, most of them richer and powerful than our own state, with their wealth and power.

These few privileged ones, are able to exploit our open arms to private investments, cheap labor and resources as they manipulate not only credit but also prices in the name of industrial development.

It did not take long before successive businessmen being nominated/awarded a seat in Parliament to represent their interests.

However, the irony of this is that it would take the form of either through pay-offs, and buying votes from unaware constituency and yet get to "Bunge" Parliament as though one was popularly elected.

Opponents through the use of money (pesa) could be silenced, so as to lets someone be nominated(pseudo)unopposed to "Bunge".

In a capitalist situation, where "pesa" speaks more louder than anything else including the truth, these things are not unimaginable.

Already today, the state of corruption and all kinds of "Magendo" in Kenya has become alarming. Some people try to justify these in terms of rapid social changes.

Moreover, we know better, that the system allows such developments since what matters is not what you know but whom you know. Not your "rights" but how much bribe you can give. In the second decade of the millennium, we were still crying loud about unending corruption..

How in the world or in Africa can one justify the selling or storing of hundreds bags of maize (waiting for prices to rise) while thousands of men, women(old and young) starve to death.

At the same time, how does one justify having millions of Kenyan shillings in a foreign bank, where one goes for extraordinary shopping and siesta, while the economy goes down, creating endless pain and misery to millions of people; yet, who and deny that this is not a reality in Kenya of 2020 and beyond.

Mzee Kenyatta used to say that "Dudu au Kuku Ameingia" katika vishwa via Wengine: Sure the presence of foreign bodies-insects or demons is the minds of some, continues to generate poverty for the Kenyan masses.

Sometimes you hear things about our nation which when you face them you doubt if truly Kenya is where it ought to be. Take a visit to former National Parks, some of the former pinkish tourist bastions , in some of these you will find yourself out of place if you are brownish African.

Go to the coast of the Kenya and small colonies of pink tycoons will surprise if not scare your Uzalendo "National Pride" out of you.

You see, to some rich Kenyans who intermingle and do business and even own a certain amount of shares in these places, the shock of the ordinary Kenyan or even the mere discrimination in his own land does not scare them.

Yet, if one chooses to straighten things up with the authorities, their efforts end up in shame to discover that in the first place they went where by their class standards they did not belong.

Things can even get worse and one would find themselves face to face with the law, for interfering with the tourist industry, the nation's second biggest earner of foreign exchange, which brings almost half of a million visitors annually.

Therefore, because the country needs the money, the leisure our people could enjoy, which used to be enjoyed by the pink foreigners, still continues to be their domain, creating a lot of money for their foreign country's investors as they exploit our national beauty.

8 SOCIALIST ALTERNATIVES

There is nothing new in the mention of African socialism in Kenya: after all it is mentioned all over the Third World, where people are struggling with socio-economic transformations.

The pre-independent Kenyan struggle was very much based on socialist ideology. Interesting enough the Session Paper #10 which for some time seems to have been shelved, was an "African Socialist Manifesto".

The recent K.A.N.U .election manifesto seemed to me to be based on a more socialist construction of the goals of the Kenyan society (See Ujamaa Wa Kiafrika na Jinsi Unaugohusiana na Mpango wa Kenya, 1965).

By socialist alternative, we mean a real mobilization of the masses for a major socio-economic transformation. This will have to focus on raising the standards of living for the majority , the poor masses of the people living in rural regions of the country.

This will halt the continuing senseless accumulation of capital that has for the last 47 years characterized our national leadership and bring an end to the economic dependence that our corporate and transnational capitalism has been based on and even nurtured.

African Socialism, unlike Capitalist Maendeleo grows out of the concern with equitable distribution of wealth, social justice and in favor of the interest of the poor people, workers and students in our country.

In 1980/90s we saw several "bills or motions favoring the Poor and Landless Squatters" being mercilessly defeated in Parliament .

At the same time the banning of the Civil Workers Union one of the strongest (workers) labor movements in the country.

The University of Nairobi/Kenyatta University were pressured with excessive government control, so as to silence student grievances and lately a complete overhaul of the student leadership.

To the Western advisers and so called "experts" such signs of discontent were seen to be inspired by "foreign ideologies", (a term vaguely defined) and need to be strongly controlled with harshest measures possible regardless of the abuses of the "human rights" of our people to peacefully protests.

All the talk in the Western press or in our foreign owned press were concerned with lingering tribalism, e.g. the Kikuyu v. the Luo or divisions of the Kikuyu of North v. Kikuyu of the South was nothing, but cosmetic journalist pastime.

The banning of Gema, or other ethnic unions, was useless unless the land these bought in the name of their people or the wealth or capital they built (which they could be legally required to distribute justly and equitably), ended up in the hands of foreign investors and companies.

In Kenya, whether we like it or not, or whether we deny it or not, we've created a class problem. "Matajiri na Maskini"(the rich and the poor) have become two increasingly growing divisions in our society.

As the nation strides beyond 2000 A.D. we find ourselves getting deeper and deeper into the transnational capitalism.

Kenya was the first African nation contrary its non-alignment stature to rally behind the U.S. boycott of Moscow Games,

Moscow still remained a leading trade partner with full diplomatic relations) which hurt our own people than it did the U.S. (of course as a part of the support Kenya may have gotten some needed cash).

Further, withan ever threatening neighbor, Somalia, Both were at one time packed together as base or facility "military allies of the U.S.".

Despite, its denial of giving a military base, the report from U.S. capital suggests no difference between the facilities or bases, they are all military in purpose.

These two moves, especially the last one, did probably accord Kenya certain benefits, either F-5 jet fighters to boost our armed forces and/or maize/wheat grains to combat hunger.

But for these to be means of neutralizing the orbit or Moscow, as U.S. may have wanted, was to involve the country into "super powers struggle" which the nation could not afford. Just as we could not afford to be in conflict with our other neighbor and then Soviet supported Ethiopia

Tanzania seems to shun our moves and Uganda seems to question our intentions and Somalia kept wondering how it can get some land compromises at the coastline border at the Indian Ocean.

Capitalist as a path for Development seems to be questionable, the longer the system continues the more it might dig its own grave.

Yet socialist construction faces many obstacles in Kenya, since capitalist "Matajiri" class created by the colonial economic minority (before they went undercover like mole-rats; into roots of our economy) will fight such a development with brutal hostility. These have a lot to lose in a society with a more just and equitable distribution of wealth ,including land..

It will not be uncommon for such people to employ anti-communist and foreign ideologies propaganda, economic blockades and political subversion and even inspire ethnic-hatred or conflicts (which colonialist used to enjoy and called "tribal warfare)" to prevent a truly socialist transformation of a unified and more just and peaceful society.

But if the capitalist reforms continue to benefit the ruling class, the privileged few and their compatriots, there will be no other alternative to capitalist Maendeleo but to look for a socialist option: which will listen to the cry of the poor and the underprivileged.

Such a move or attempt might face suffering and partial failures but these are characteristics profound for a radical socio-cultural transformation.

A socialist "mixed economy" seems probably better for the Kenya of 2000, rather than our capitalist "mixed economy" as we prefer to call it.

We got a new government under President Daniel Moi, who had taken leadership after the death of the founding father of the nation Mzee Jomo Kenyatta. Moi moved from being a man of the people to the dictator a one party state had made him to be.

We were surely in trouble when our Parliament, which was supposed to be the people's voice, failed to legislate laws and programs favoring the majority - the poor people in our country, most of them living in rural areas.

Kenyan parliament was supposed to scrutinize the governments bureaucratic actions and watch over that nations treasury. When this body was threatened by arbitrary arrests (as in the past) for debates in the chambers, the voice of the people was silenced.

The immunity from such arrests was abused and the whole national assembly become just a mere bureaucratic subordinate of the civil service, which forced the masses to seek other means of expression.

Let us not forget Uganda before Amin was considered civilized but what happened under Amin was unimaginable. Kenya is not Uganda or any other country like Equatorial Guinea nor

Central African Republic which underwent brutal dictatorship and mass brutalization, but yet all these countries were" considered civilized and considered stable" until the unexpected took place.

By its very nature the capitalist system seems explosive, and for Kenya to be based on it is our greatest concern, since the explosion might take place any time messing up years of hard work.

9 CONCLUSION

It was indeed a privilege for me as a social science graduate student to address this honorable Student and Civil Servants' Assembly, composed of those that later who influenced much of the Public Policies of our great nation (then and) in 21st century.

At that time, I strongly felt that, as a Kenyan Mwenyenchi,(citizen-nation owner) I believe it is my God given "human right" to get involved in the decisions and reflection of the future of our Kenyan society in the next Decades.

In order to contribute to the theme of the Conference, "Kenya Towards Year 2000", I had based my discussion on the ideological aspects of socio-economic development of our nation.

Therefore, was appropriate for me to ask the often asked question of nation building, "Tutainjenga Vipi Nchi Yetu?" How are we going to build our Nation towards year 2050 and beyond.?

Finally, let me ask again "Tutainjenga Vipi Nchi Yetu?" How are we going to build our nation?

It seems to me that this is a question that every Kenyan citizen should be allowed to answer. I happen to believe that "thought is action". People are rational human beings.

We do not just act for the sake of acting. Maendeleo (Modernization, Development or Progress) is an ideology as well as social relations.

Kenyans need guidance to the sort of society as a united people we should be building. For us in 1980/1990s the K.A.N.U .Election manifesto said it well, but never followed by deeds, **"ours should be a more just society ,with equal distribution of wealth and freedom of expression as human being".**

The development should be African, the basis on which true unity can be realized in terms of our communalism, socialist development should be our guiding ideology to build the peaceful, sharing and loving society we need.

Equality and Freedom: should structure our social, economic, cultural and political relations in which everybody gets an equal share of the fruits of Uhuru.

Capitalism and the transnational corporations, with the "Matajiri" class being produced by its presence, should continually be subjected to a constructive critique until a true transformation of our society is possible.

As to international relations or participation in world economy, ours would probably be a "mixed path", being socialist by true definition of the word, yet producing enough capital (minus the exploiting evils of western capitalism) to equally distribute to our people.

Let us actualize our national anthem.

[Ee Mungu nguvu yetu. Ilete

baraka kwetu,

Haki iwe Ngao na Ulinzi

Oh God of all creation.

Bless this Land and Nation,

Justice be our Shield and Defender.

10 REFERENCES

Kihara, Nehemy Ndirangu,

1984: Religion and Politics in the Economic Development of Kenya and Tanzania, (p. 24-33).Ph.D. Dissertation, University, Atlanta, GA

Mwaniki, H.S.K.

1982: A Pre-Colonial History of Chuka of Mount Kenya a 1400-1968 Ph.D. Thesis of Dalhorsie University, Canada.

Ochieng, W.R.

1985: A History of Kenya, London, O.U.P.

Spear, T.

1981: Kenya's Past, London, Longman.

ABOUT THE AUTHOR

The Revd. Prof. Dr. Nehemy Ndirangu Kihara was born in Nanyuki in Laikipia County of Kenya, East Africa.

He was educated at Timau in Meru County and Nairobi before graduating with a Licentiate of Theological Education from St. Paul's University (United Theological College), Limuru in Kiambu County. He holds a Bachelor of Theology (B.Th.) in Biblical Literature and Geographic History from Christian International College.

He graduated with honors and attained a Master of Divinity (M.Div.) in Social Ethics, Psychology of Religion and Counseling, from the Interdenominational Theological Center at the Clark Atlanta University Complex.

He also attained a Doctor of Philosophy (Ph.D.) in Anthropology, Sociology of Religion and Political Science from Emory University.

As an Investigative Journalist and Radio Broadcaster this Independent Publisher hosted a weekend English and still hosts a weekly Swahili Community Show for Sagal Radio Services at WATB 1420 AM Station in Decatur, GA.

As an Interdisplinary Educator he taught Security Management and Police Studies for the Institute of Peace and Security Studies, (now known as the Department of Security and Correctional Science) of Kenyatta University in Nanyuki Campus, where he was the Coordinator of Humanities and Examinations Officer.

The Author also taught Introductory Psychology, Sociology, Criminal Procedure and Law of Evidence, Intelligence-Led Policing, Public Administration and General Management Principles among other units at the Nyeri and Embu Campuses.

He was an Adjunct Professor of Sociology/ Social Sciences at the Atlanta Campus of Saint Leo University, Tampa, Fl. Taught such courses as Anthropology, Sociology, and Criminal Justice units as Social Theory, Drugs and Society, Marriage and Family, Research Methods, Human Behavior, among others He was an Adjunct Professor of Ethics at the Georgia Campus (Henry Medical Center) of the College of Health, University of St. Francis, Joliet, Ill.,

The Author was also the founding Moderating Bishop of the Ujamaa Nomadic Church -Without Borders, as a new church- mission initiative in US. He had also been an Urban Renewal/ Organizing Pastor of Beth Salem United Presbyterian Church, Columbus, Georgia. He served as an International Missionary in California, Iowa and New York, under the Mission to US program of the Presbyterian Church, USA.

As a Senior Lecturer at Kenyatta University, the Author taught African Culture, Belief Systems, Social Theory and Research Methods units in the Department of Philosophy and Religious Studies and also in the Department of Sociology. He was also an Activist Educator, who fought for academic freedom and excellence, which led to his unfair dismissal by the government which controlled the public universities and educational institutions.

Reverend Professor Ndirangu Kihara started his career a high school teacher and principal at Muthithi Secondary School, and then an ordained Church Minister of Muthithi Parish and the Stated Clerk of the wider Murang'a Presbytery of the Presbyterian Church of East Africa.

BLUERGREEN PUBLISHERS